Perception Vs Reality
In Culture

Perception Vs Reality In Culture

A CLOSER LOOK AT THE WAY WE LIVE

Marlene Louis Blyden

Author of:
My Daughters and Me: Laughing All the Way

To order additional copies of this book, contact:
Xlibris Corporation
1-888-795-4274
www.Xlibris.com
Orders@Xlibris.com
118510

Contents

Dedication

To my wonderful, precious daughters, Myla-Danae and Malaeya, I say thank you for being you. This book is dedicated to you, my baby girls! May you always live your lives to the fullest, the way that the Lord intended you to do. I love you.

I also dedicate this book in loving memory of my mother Marie Lumina LaRocque Louis who passed away in April 2012. Her love of reading and literature has been a constant encouragement to me and the remainder of her family. She will be missed, but her legacy of being a dedicated wife and mother will live on in her children, grandchildren, and generations to come. I love you, Mama!

~ Marlene Louis Blyden

Introduction

How often do we look at ourselves and others around us and truly take note? I am not talking about comparing ourselves to each other. Rather, I am referring to us looking at the many ways in which we are alike and other areas in which we are so different. We might say to ourselves, "This person is weird" or "how she speaks, interacts, and dresses are strange." These might all be legitimate reactions but do we ever wonder, "I must seem strange to others too." Yes, there are people who, no matter where they live or what part of the world they come from, will seem completely "off." They do not fit any societal norms or rules. They call themselves nonconformist, or eccentrics, or even mavericks. These are not the individuals I had in mind when I asked the previous question, though. Everyone has a background, history and culture. Without a shadow of a doubt we are all *unique.* Many of those differences are clearly seen in the same culture or ethnicity but magnified when placed in the context of a new culture. If at all possible, some people would choose to carry some of, none of, or all of their background to wherever they live.

Too often, we do not take the time to be introspective or self-aware. We see behaviors and events every day and think nothing much of them. Some individuals may be bothered, disturbed, or otherwise confused by others' actions but may not know how to respond appropriately to them. Looking at others through the lenses of curiosity, or to acquire knowledge, is an added bonus to our daily lives, in my view. I tend to do the latter quite often, sometimes intentionally and at other times automatically. In this book, I discuss my observations and personal feelings on certain subjects. I can speak only for myself, so feel free to disagree with my observations, but more likely than not, I believe you will agree with my analysis. My views are not meant to be "heavy" or too deep. Nevertheless, the subject areas discussed here are truly relevant and fascinating. Read on you will see for yourself.

Today, for the most part living in the United States is second nature to me. Yet, every so often, I realize that I still need to adjust to some aspects of the system. Keep in mind I am writing from my perspective with respect to individuals, cultures, and nations. None of us had any power in choosing where we were born or how we were raised. However, the fact remains that we choose to be who we are today.

One of my main goals in this book is to help you to take a few moments and see yourself and your culture through someone else's eyes. You may think to yourself, "Why should I care about others people's perceptions of me?" On the flip side, I ask, Why should they care about your perceptions of them?" You see, in a civilized society, our attitudes and behaviors affect other people. The old saying is still true, *no one is an island.* I also want you to see yourself not only as your "own person," but as an individual from a particular family and cultural background. Yes, it is possible! If you do, you will discover indeed your culture is jam-packed with pros and cons, and contradictions, just like the other person's. No one chose their family of origin, ethnicity, culture or country of birth. Therefore, the onus is on each individual to make the best of their given circumstances. It is OK to hang on to the positive, and let go of the negative aspects of your upbringing. Likewise, when you find yourself residing in a new country/culture you do not have to adopt all attitudes and behaviors you see practiced there.

In this book, *Perception Vs Reality In Culture* I highlight some of the main observations that I have made after traveling and living in different parts of the world, as a participant and observer. I use satire (not so much sarcasm), and some levity to help paint a clear picture of my experiences and observations of specific aspects of human nature and behavior, specifically in the Dominican and American cultures. Isn't it a great feeling when you are able to laugh and learn at the same time? Sometimes a good, old belly laugh, even at yourself is what you need to get you out of a dark or down mood. So, beloved laugh if you have to!

We sometimes take ourselves too seriously. Don't misunderstand me now. It goes without me belaboring the point that there are times that serious occasions require us to be focused and intense. As Ecclesiastes 3:1-8 teaches, there is a time for everything under the sun. There is a time to laugh and a time to cry. So making light of every life situation is definitely not my motto or advice. Hopefully, a new perspective and a little inspiration will jump out of the pages of: *Perception Vs Reality In Culture* into your thought process.

Chapter One

You Did Not Choose Your Family of Origin

We choose our acquaintances, mates/spouses, friends, homes, jobs but not our families. Oh no! Sometimes we wish we could trade our families in for new ones just like we would an old car. A real life *dream come true* for some of us, right? How many of us would really change our family of origin if we could? If yes, what family would you want to be born into instead? Don't answer too quickly now. Most people (I am guessing) would automatically zoom in, like a highly accurate radar on the negative aspects of their families when they think about their answers. Would you like to be from a famous, wealthy, well-known, or well-connected family? Take a closer look at any of the families that popped into your mind, and before long, you will discover that they have the biggest scandals and problems you could imagine. Regardless of the era of the family you chose, they had their serious challenges too.

Take a trip back to biblical times and study the families of Abraham, David and Lot. Abraham lied and said his wife Sarah was his sister when she was indeed his wife. Look at King David's family. David had one of his soldiers (Uriah the Hittite) killed in battle so he could have his (Uriah's) wife, Bathsheba for himself. Lot's wife turned to a pillar of salt due to her disobedience. As if that was not horrendous enough, Lot's daughters got him drunk and conceived children by him (Genesis 19: 30-37). Undoubtedly, these attitudes and actions are repulsive and repugnant in any sane society, regardless of the era.

Sometimes it seems from the outside looking in that everyone's family is united, prospering, and doing so well while ours seem to be in ruins or constantly taking steps backward. Through the years, families everywhere have been plagued with deceit, lies, greed, envy, strife and major dysfunction. You can go on to study families during the Victorian era down to modern times, you name it, and they had serious issues. They had their positive characteristics on one hand and *serious drama* on the other!

Thankfully, even when an entire family is lost or fails, there is sometimes one individual who stands out and shines like a star. There have been great examples of individuals with integrity and unshaken character. One such outstanding example is Job from the Bible. He suffered so much loss and heartache yet he remained faithful to his God. If you are not familiar with his story or need to gain some encouragement today, go read the book of Job in the Bible. Everyone of us can gain so much strength from the life of this godly man.

Born and raised in a strict, Christian, Dominican family has shaped my life in many ways. However, for as long as I can remember, I always had an interest in learning about peoples and different cultures. I longed to expand my knowledge about human behavior as well. As a young child, despite my limited exposure to cultural experiences and behavior, my interest never faded. I never expected to end up residing in the United States. Nevertheless, living in the biggest melting pot or (salad bowl if you prefer) and freest country in the world has afforded me this chance, so I am jumping in with both feet. To this end, I pursued and completed an undergraduate degree in Psychology and a graduate degree in Counseling (talk about studying human behavior)! Surely, studying culture and human behavior cannot be complete or half as interesting by merely reading it from a book. No way! We have to live it.

Let us not forget God allowed each person to be born into his or her own "individual" family. Moreover, EACH one of us must strive to live out His purpose for our lives no matter how we may feel about our family members. At times, it seems to some like fighting a losing battle, but we are who we are because God allowed us to be born at a certain time in history to specific parents. We also need to realize and embrace the fact that when we become adults, with or without a family of our own, we decide the type and frequency of interaction we have with our parents, siblings, cousins, etc. These relationships are dynamic; they change over time. Yes having family close or being in touch with our family of origin is a wonderful aspect of our lives, providing that they are healthy relationships. We could avoid much of our heartache and unnecessary angst if we live with appropriate boundaries in our daily lives. As rational, functioning adults, with loads of common sense we are capable of deciding on whom we want to spend our time and energy. Being thoughtless, insensitive or selfish is not the intent here. Remember we can all benefit from our past experiences with family members. All of these events did not happen by chance. So, don't allow all this invaluable insights that you have gathered over time go to waste. Every one of us must make the very best of our experiences, and maybe add some richness and depths to someone else's life.

Different People, Same Family

Though our families are different in so many ways from our neighbor's, some similarities are still very evident. Here are some of the major categories that I have created based on my observations of human behavior. *Disclaimer: these are not official psychological disorders or terms or any other theories currently used, as far as I know.* These are all original problem categories that I came up with after much observation. Thankfully, the majority of people are sensible and 'normal.' Furthermore, this section does not pertain to people who have displayed those behaviors or attitudes from time to time. Rather, it refers to those who do so almost all the time. These individuals are chronic and habitual offenders. They are known by all family members for being this way. Which one of these can you find in your family of origin (parents, siblings, aunts, uncles, cousins)? I hope none. Don't be stunned if you see someone you know in one or a combination of these categories. Beware, that someone may be you!

+ The "nonstop talker" goes from one family member to another. They will blab to whoever is around to listen to their stories. These individuals just have the "gift of gab." Driven by their incessant desire they seem to make the time to spread gossip. It makes them feel great that there is tragic or bad news to spread. They will make the news graver than the reality. Exaggeration is never far from their lips. If you want to find out what is going on at any given time with anyone, just call them. Much of their stories are plain falsehoods anyway. The following is not recommended by this author: Sometimes people use these individuals as cheap mindless entertainment after a long dull day knowing that their stories may be far from the truth. The nonstop talker is the embodiment of "busybody."

+ The "woe is me" kind always has a sob story. In their world, things are always *doom and gloom*. The glass is not even half empty; it is broken, cannot be repaired, and therefore can hold no water. Their brightest mood is melancholy. They will bring your mood down if you are not careful. Even when you are well-intentioned they will reject your encouragement, sometimes overtly and at other times in a more subtle way. If you try to tell them to look on the sunny side, they will say, "Sure. Things are great with you. I am glad for you. As for me, I don't know what I am going to do. It is just a mess." There is hardly a bright day for them, just OK days. Even when things are looking great in their lives, they cannot enjoy it because they anticipate that the peace and quiet is not real or will not last. Surely, tragedy is around the bend.

+ The "self-centered/my life is always perfect" type lives most of their lives in denial of what is really going on. Their reality is so warped that they believe the stories they tell about how great their spouses and children are all the time. They do not really care to hear about you and your issues. They prefer to talk about their life, which in their mind is the only significant one out there. Personally, I have no problem with the optimist. I wish we had more optimists around. However, these people are not optimists although they may delude themselves and others into thinking that. They are living in the world they have created in their minds, the world they wish existed. It is truly sad. Reality escapes them, and they love it so. Knowing that their stories are not true will not uplift your spirit; it will do just the opposite. If you choose to buy into all their hype, their blatant disregard for others and superiority complex, be forewarned you will be left confused and asking yourself, "Really?!"

+ The "secretive/avoidant type" is hardly available when you need them or when you just want to just say a simple hello. They do not want to talk about their life, and they surely do not want to hear about yours. They will stay away from family functions or gatherings as much as they can. It could be a small part of their personality, maybe an introvert who prefers to be alone and avoid social events or the more sinister version who may not want to be bothered, period. They deal with their issues and prefer that no one knows what is going on in their part of the universe. The great thing about these individuals is that they do not spread gossip and are able to keep confidences if they will take a moment to converse with others. However, they are notoriously unreliable and undependable in terms of how much they will do for you and when. Therefore, you should learn to treat them as such and not expect too much from them.

+ The "know-it-all" type can be rather obnoxious. They irritate others to no end. They will talk and are oblivious to others' uncomfortable reactions to what they have to say. If you have a problem, they have the answers. Still, their lives may be in total disorder, and they do not have any answers to solve their own problems. They know about and possess the latest electronic gadgets. They are experts on the domestic and world news, newest inventions, best diets, and exercise techniques. They are the *jacks-of-all-trades* and, of course, master of none. They will make it no secret if they really know more about a subject matter than you do. They feel important and have an inflated sense of self and importance. They will rarely say, "I have never heard or seen such and such." If it is out there, they are aware of it. And, believe me; they have so deluded themselves that they actually deem their opinions and perspectives are far superior to those of anyone else. They loathe rejection or someone telling them or even insinuating that they may be wrong. They may vacillate from approachable to aggressive very quickly. Dear reader, tread lightly around such an individual.

+ The "lacking discretion" type is like a loose cannon, truly unpredictable. They can be a lot of fun to have around. They are free-spirited, open, and compassionate. They are the huggers, talkers, and sometime listeners. They are social butterflies. You can see their loud colors from a mile way. On the flip side, they often lack self-control and may overindulge. They may tend to drink too freely. From time to time, a curse word or two will fly out of their mouths. People will go to them and expect them to say what is on their minds, good, bad, or ugly. They are nonviolent overall. They will be apologetic about their behavior, but don't expect any noticeable changes at the next family gathering.

+ The "people-pleaser" type wants to make everyone happy. They do not want to offend anyone. Pretty soon, they become the family "pushover" if they are not careful. You will find them more empathetic to others' needs and situations. They will also try to be peacemakers. People will turn to them for a sympathetic ear. They will hold their tongues and try to be tactful and think before they speak. They do not want to take sides since they want to make everyone happy. However, in the end, they are so torn within themselves as to whether they said the right words, if someone is mad at them, or if they did the right thing. They spend nights tossing and turning over decisions they made. They rehearse their conversations with others before they see them. Persons with this particular weakness mean well. But they also feel a profound emptiness deep down. Therefore, they will try to fill that void with other people's admiration. Bottom-line: they want people to like them. But in the end, they make themselves miserable when they realize that they cannot please everyone. They need to be more confident and act independently without others' approval. They should follow their instincts and stick to their values, regardless of whether it is popular with the other family members. What is the probability of such individuals acting is such a rational manner? Slim to none.

✦ The "faulty fault-finder" is criticism exemplified. These individuals will find fault with anything and everything and anyone. They will criticize your dress, speech, food, family. They will even make disparaging comments about your children's physical features. They will hold nothing back. Of course, no one with one ounce of self-respect and sensitivity will want to be around them. Nothing meets their standards, and I am sure not even they can articulate those said standards. Deep down, they are miserable, pitiful people. Ask yourself, "What kind of person takes the time to bring others down, constantly?" Answer: "Not a happy, contented soul." They may seem tough and are truly abrasive to all on the outside, but they are really pathetic souls inside.

✦ The "compete-with-you-at-all-costs" type is never satisfied with what they own or possess. They will have one car or house design today but see another family member with another model, which they think is better, and pretty soon will find a way to acquire that object or one similar. If you go on vacation to a certain place, they will follow suit and head there as well. They will post similar comments and pictures of themselves and their children on Facebook and other social media sites. They are in deep credit card and other debt. They will use credit cards until they are maxed out and apply for new ones. They will have no shame in asking family members to loan them money for new possessions, which we all know they do not need. They are so superficial that even your baby's name is not off limits. These individuals will envy the name of your child. And true to twisted form, they will name their new baby something similar or, for the truly narcissistic type, the exact name. This person will try to outdo all of their siblings or children. Even after all these acquisitions, they will keep on looking for more to acquire. It is not uncommon to find them working two or three jobs just to sign up their children in all the same activities that their family members' children may be in. This is a truly insecure and unhappy person.

Different colors, stripes, and personalities abound within our families. Nevertheless, I say God chose them to be in our families and vice versa, so we have no choice but to accept them. This is not to say that we have to condone their behavior. Instead, it means we need to accept them as part of our family of origin. Period. We have our lives to lead, so we should not use their negative actions to impede our personal growth and lasting joy. If you are the one family member hindering others' peace of mind, then you have some serious decisions to make towards change and growth, if you so desire. It is better for you and everyone in your family if you are willing to soar way above all this mediocrity!

Inevitably, family members will hurt us. Oftentimes, we find it the hardest to accept or forgive when it is a parent that is causing us the embarrassment or pain. Some parents will continue to treat their child the same way whether that child is five or fifty-five. A hard pill to swallow indeed! These parents demonstrate *conditional* love and acceptance towards their young and adult children. Contrast these attitudes to children in families whose parents dote on them, show attention, and try not to intentionally hurt their feelings. Their children love to be around them, even when they are adults. They go out of their way to bring the grandchildren to visit them as much as possible. What an absolute blessing! I want to be the latter parent for sure. How about you?

Chapter Two

Life Is So Different Here

As you read through this book, you will likely conclude that I am writing about my experiences often as an outsider looking in. In other words, America was once a completely foreign land to me. I am extremely thankful that the United States is currently my permanent home. If you were born in this country, or your family tree traces its roots here for two or more generations, you may think of certain core American traditions, holidays, and occasions as just part of life. No problems with that. However, for someone who is new to this country, seemingly mundane routine events like going to your child's Little League baseball games, volunteering at the local homeless shelter, or Boys and Girls type clubs can be viewed in a different light. As most foreigners looking in, these events immediately stand out. From where I am sitting, thus far, the vast majority of my impressions and reactions to the abovementioned traditions have been positive.

Anyone with a basic understanding and respect for the United States would appreciate the significance of key days like Veterans Day, Memorial Day, Independence Day, and Thanksgiving Day, even if they do not understand the entire history behind these observations. Museums, galleries, amusement parks, fast food restaurants, county fairs, and so much more that comprise the American culture are not experienced by many other countries. If they do enjoy such events and traditions, they would be on a much smaller scale. The new immigrant who wants to make America his or her new home will try his or her best to learn about these events and participate as much as possible. For sure, the cultural experiences are rich, diverse, and exciting here!

It is noteworthy to add that people of certain ethnicities and cultures have such thriving communities in the United States that they do not even need to learn English to be successful here. Examples of these communities include China Town in New York and other Cities, or Little Havana in Miami, and Little Italy in other cities, just to name a few. Their communities look very much like the countries they left behind. They see their culture everywhere. They enjoy their dishes, and hear their music and language all the time. Therefore, their adjustment in many ways is not such a huge change. They will have vastly different experiences when they leave the familiarity of their communities or enclaves and branch out into other parts of their cities or towns. If they choose to live and work outside the areas of their predominant ethnicity or culture they will be like the rest of us who assimilate and try to survive. Outside the comfort and security of their communities they will certainly experience some level of "culture shock."

Food

Unless you have lived overseas or traveled to another country, you may never grasp the significant differences that can be found in culture. When I arrived here, it was a lot for my senses to absorb at once. It was truly overwhelming. After I got over the initial culture shock, I gradually started to process this "new world," if you will. So many things stood out to me right away; others became evident over time. Food remains one of the great ingredients which adds such meaningful texture to the great *American Pie.*

American cuisine is truly special. It consists of contributions from many cultures and ethnicities. It is indeed a "melting pot" of culinary diversity. Contrast this to Dominica, where we mainly cook local Dominican cuisine. I can tell you Dominican cooking is the top in my book. Every time I return home, family and friends expect me to request pizza or burgers, but I do not. No sir! I love their surprise expressions when I asked for only local foods. There is nowhere in the world you can find Dominican food except for Dominica the *Nature Isle of the Caribbean.* Therefore, why would I not enjoy as much as I can when I do not have access to such savory foods on a daily basis. By the way in case you missed my not so subtle hint, this author, Marlene Louis Blyden highly recommends the consumption of authentic Dominican cuisine! In order to enjoy those mouth-watering and palette thrilling delights your next vacation should be in Dominica.

Dominicans consume mainly fresh, locally-grown fruits, vegetables, chicken, and meats. You can find your dinner and other meals in your own backyard or even your neighbors or relative's backyard. Every day, people in different villages can be seen heading "down by the bay," where they get fresh fish, from the local fishermen. Then they take the fish home to clean, prepare and consume.

I remember, as a child fresh fish was desired by most Dominicans although it was plentiful in many villages. That's a beneficial tradition to maintain. I really miss hearing those conch shells and "running down by the bay." The villagers listened for the conch shell, which indicates that the fishermen were back with their catch. You may be asking, "How do you prepare this fish straight from the ocean, daily?" There are several ways of doing so. First, you have to use a sharp knife to scale and clean the insides of the fish and wash them well. Caution: you may bruise and cut your fingers and hands with the sharp fins or maybe the knife if you are not careful. I know the fins of certain fish do cut. Ouch! I cut my fingers several times. Not fun at all. After the cleaning, then use fresh herbs to "season" them. Most people allow the seasoning to sink in for a while maybe a couple hours before they cook the fish. The main ways of fish cooking that I remember are fish broth, fried fish, and smoke fish, steam (gravy or cook on the stovetop. When well done, fish is scrumptious, healthy food. Oh, do not forget that the fish is not cooked alone. You need ground provision like tania, dasheen, green bananas, rice, peas or beans, and vegetable with it. No, it is not easy to prepare all of this from *scratch*, but no one really thought of this preparation in terms of the time and energy it would take to have a meal on the table. It was the order of the day. There was no other way around it. If you want to eat, you do the work, as unappealing as it may sound.

Dominicans will rear their chicken and pluck and cook them as well. The same procedure applies to cows, sheep, pigs, rabbits, goats and sometime ducks. No, these animals are not pets! They are meals! If a family doesn't have these animals, they will get them from a local farmer or local market. Overall, the procedure is still the same. The person needs to clean and prepare and cook these appetizing meats. I am sure there are vegetarians on the islands, or vegans who eat absolutely no meat or meat by-products. However, I can say with certainty that the majority of residents are meat-eaters. Mountain Chicken (*Crapaud*) is one of the most appetizing or sort after dishes on the island.

Contrast these types of preparations which could be considered to be: old-fashioned, outdated, primitive or completely foreign to the methods used by the majority of Americans. In the United States, you can find fresh and organic foods at the farmers' market or in different sections at the local supermarket. Still, the availability of any processed and frozen foods far outnumbers those of fresh foods. Growing up, we had some canned goods but no frozen vegetables or TV diners. These words did not exist in my vocabulary. I found out about them after moving to America. All non-alcoholic juices that I can think of except for the occasional soda, were freshly squeezed. Juice from fresh orange, pineapple, grapefruit, cherries, papaya, guava, soursop, lime, lemon, passion fruit, and the list goes on, can be prepared by the average child at home. In most homes here, you pick up your premade and ready-to-drink juice, soda/pop at the local supermarket or corner store. In the United States, you can also find almost any food or vegetable ready to cook or already cooked. Just pop it in the oven or microwave and voila, Let's eat! Not in Dominica. You have to harvest your food or buy it from the market and then prepare it the way you choose. In terms of overall health benefits and nutrition, I'd stick my neck out there, go out on a limb and calmly state that freshly caught and prepared is the way to go!

Another observation I made in the United States, which I never saw in Dominica, is some people's obsession with food. Everyone has their favorite meal, drink, snack, or desert. They can talk about food for hours on end. Some people will go overboard if they do not have their doughnuts, coffee, sweets, chocolate, or favorite drink at the very instant that they feel the craving. They might just lose it completely, and their day is ruined. Food can be found literally, everywhere. In the United States, ironically the people who seem the most obsessed are not starving by any stretch of the imagination. Yet they will not be satisfied knowing it is all at their disposal. They want more. I realize that this issue goes deeper than just wanting food. Therefore, I will not flesh out this matter much further at this time. Sometimes, I say to myself. "This person is acting like they never saw food before." In other poorer or developing countries, people are thankful for the meals they receive and will hardly make a fuss if they do not have a particular food or drink on any given day. They are just thankful to have a meal. Period.

At the office, for breakfast, people bring in doughnuts and coffee. Potlucks are very popular here. People love participating in potluck meals at work, church, and so many other settings. At a potluck each attendee brings a meal or drink, whether home-cooked or bought at the store. The host usually provides the location and cutlery and sometimes a dish as well. My friends love to participate. They look forward to these occasions. This makes sense. These are great occasions for socializing and small talk with friends, co-workers and other acquaintances, but sometimes I just do not feel comfortable eating meals prepared by people

I hardly know. Consequently, you will find me eating fruits or drinking juice at the potluck, rather than sampling every dish on the table.

I still refuse to eat doughnuts and coffee for breakfast, not just for the health reasons but they just do not taste good in the morning. After all, it took me several years to get used to eating pancakes and waffles with syrup for breakfast. They are still not my favorites but I indulge occasionally. The breakfast foods I enjoy the most are my Johnny Cake otherwise known as Bakes. For those of my readers who are not familiar with this must-have breakfast. It is similar to doughnut, without the hole or sugar. It also looks like pancakes but firmer and thicker in size. We have this with freshly ground hot cocoa and smoked herring or salt fish, cucumber, and tomato salad. Just thinking about this makes my tummy rumble and my mouth water a little. "Fish for breakfast?" you ask. Believe me, it is good, really good!

To Eat or Not To Eat

I never heard of food recalls until I came to live in the United States. We ate all kinds of foods with no kind of Department of Agriculture to orally regulate or monitor the foods we consumed. Yes there is a department responsible for food handling permit for qualified candidates. Here in the United States, The Department of Agriculture (USDA) has that role. The primary purpose of the USDA is to make sure that all American food that is manufactured and consumed is safe, nutritious and sustainable. The USDA thus establishes and enforces regulations about food handling, preparation and manufacturing. It seeks to find ways to make crops healthier, such as growing certain hybrids or reducing pesticide use. It also works with farmers to develop techniques that enable the farmers to produce crops without injury in an efficient and renewable way. I agree the USDA is necessary and does a good job protecting the consumer.

In Dominica, some of the major stores and small shops alike sold expired products; yes, I said "expired" products at discounted prices. Consumers rushed to buy those products. If there are laws on the books against such practices by stores, these laws are not enforced. Therefore, checking the dates of items for sale is not high on the priority list of store owners. There is something to say about God's mercy and protection on the poor and uninformed in this case, because this is a dangerous practice indeed! It is different in the US, store owners are a bit more careful with the products they place on their shelves.

Buildings and Infrastructure

The Caribbean has two seasons—the dry season and the hurricane season (rainy season). Therefore, the homes are generally built accordingly to withstand both seasons, which can be brutal at times. Some of the homes are concrete made with cement, sand, and small pebbles, known as "chipping," with steel reinforcement and little pebbles with cement. The builders dig several feet in the ground to construct the foundation of the home. There are also wooden houses with aluminum covers know as galvanize. These houses there are built to last. They are built to withstand strong winds and heavy rain, which will pour down at some point every year. Smart home builders usually build houses on pillars and off the ground to prevent flooding.

In the United States, most states expect four seasons: spring, summer, autumn/fall and winter every year. Many homes are completely flat and built on ground level on a slab, with no digging for the foundation. Furthermore, some of the homes here are built of wood, or similar product with vinyl sidings with no steel reinforcement. Brick homes are more expensive. Even so, many are not solid brick or stone. Instead, it is just a façade for external aesthetic purposes only. The bare bones of the homes are surprisingly weak. It doesn't give too much confidence about the durability and ability to protect life and possessions found within. This is evident when there are strong winds or tornadoes. The aftermath reveals houses peeled back, literally crushed to nothing because they were too weak or poorly constructed. No amount of reinforcement can protect against all of nature's fury. Nevertheless, in my mind, many changes need to be made in the codes and building of weak or unsafe commercial and residential buildings.

Roads and Traffic

The roads and traffic in Dominica or most of the other Caribbean countries and the highways in America bear little comparison. Most roads or highways back in the Dominica are mainly two lanes and narrow. Dominica's winding roads are narrow and many instances steep. This is all due to the mountainous and rugged terrain of the Nature Isle. Therefore great skill and concentration needs to be practiced all the time while navigating the roads on this island. In the United States, major highways are three and more lanes in either direction. The traffic congestion is much less for obvious reasons in Dominica such as the smaller population and fewer vehicles on the roads. In Dominica, traffic congestion happens mainly on the narrow roads, due to road construction and accidents but not due to the sheer amount of traffic on the road. During rush hour, as expected the volume increases. However, it is all manageable. Roads can be obstructed due to landslides and mudslides which occur after heavy rainfall. So the roads can be dangerous in certain rural areas of Dominica. However, people have learned to navigate around these obstacles somehow, unless the road is completely blocked off and no vehicles can pass through.

In many regions in the United States, mudslides/landslides may not be common occurrences. However, accidents, road rage, and other issues are prevalent and problematic to all US residents. According to the Centers for Disease Control and Prevention (CDC), in 2009, In the US alone 10,839 people were killed in alcohol-impaired driving crashes. About one third of all traffic related deaths are directly connected to the alcohol consumption of drivers. The cost of these crashes cost over five billion dollars annually. If these statistics do not shock you, then maybe you need check your pulse. It is truly unbelievable. I am sure there are drunk drivers everywhere in the world. The roads can be hazardous and tragic at any given moment anywhere, but adding drunk or impaired drivers to the list is very frightening indeed. Still, I believe the average person would prefer spacious roads and lanes, as opposed to narrow ones with deep gauges, otherwise known as precipices, alongside them. Each individual has his or her different comfort level on the roads. My gut instinct is that one should never be complacent or too relaxed while driving no matter the country. Bear in mind, just being on a motor vehicle whether you are a passenger or driver it is dangerous wherever you may be under the sun.

Noise

It can be very loud in the Caribbean, no doubt about that. Loud reggae, calypso, socca, and gospel music will blast from homes, cars, businesses, busses and other venues or locations. Noise is a part of life. People in Dominica are loud; they like to argue. You can hear the loud barks of your neighbor's dog at any hour of the day or night. This noise pollution, will be sure to disturb your late morning nap! Annoying! It is amazing to me when these same loudmouths, owners of the untrained loud dogs, who blast loud music, can be as quiet as church mice in certain situations and settings. They are able to be quiet at church, libraries, and even in the banks. In those aforementioned situations, the expectations are that people should act subdued and talk in a lower tones. If someone even makes the slightest sound at a library or bank, he or she will be sure to receive not only nasty looks but "SSSSHhhhhh" not just from the employees of these establishments but also from patrons in line or sitting waiting for service. Take it easy now. It is not that serious.

In the United States, people are also loud everywhere. Even at the library, it can be a ruckus at times. People are supposed to be studying or reading quietly at the library yet it is not uncommon to hear another person yapping away on his or her cell phone. It is not rare, rather, it is a common occurrence to see this scenario played out: a young teen or late teen young lady is snapping her chewing gum and playing with her hair and browsing social network sites. If you hang around long enough you may hear a conversation which goes something like this:

So it's like I never even saw her Facebook picture. Yeah, did you see her comment? I will upload it now, now that is so totally cool, LOL. Come on, post that one. I unfriended her already. Yes loser. Totally lame. SHM (means shaking my head).

This loud obnoxious distraction should not be happening at a library. It seems like no place is sacred or quiet anymore.

At the airport, bus stop, train station, and grocery store some people just disregard each other's personal space. They are just plain rude and inconsiderate. By the way there are rude people everywhere and in every culture. To all the inconsiderate folks: Silence is Golden, still.

What Privacy?

It is true that a large number of people in our population will do almost anything to get on a television show, any television show. Be it the *real housewives, the game show, dating show, animal show,* you name it they will not turn it down. They also, will go on television shows like Oprah and Maury and discuss the most intimate parts of their lives. Airing dirty laundry about paternity of babies, infidelity or criminal acts are not a huge deal any more. The desire for attention, celebrity, fame or a few dollars are all more important than personal pride and dignity.

It seems that in the United States some people place freely expressing their feelings and talking about their problems over privacy and anonymity. At an airport, on an airplane plane, or bus ride, at the mall, in line at grocery store, at doctors office you name it, some people will dish out to you their detailed life history before you even say 'hi' to them. It is no secret that Americans are bold and love to express themselves, whether good or bad. It seems some Americans will discuss almost any private matter at anytime. Now, I cannot tell you how much information people have given me on flights about their families and children. It is amazing. They will even show the photographs on their cell phones. Other proud parents and grandparents will show the photographs found in their wallets, without the slightest hint of hesitation. Let's not talk about Facebook and how it has taken over the lives of some individuals. They will tell everything, even the most insignificant event or thought on Facebook. People will tell the whole world if their new-born baby sneezed, if they are out buying ice-cream, or if they are just sitting on the couch looking at the ceiling. Oh, I can go on for days about the personal information you can find out about someone on the internet. Search engines like Google and Yahoo will spit out detailed information like: name, age, address, cost of home, names on title of home, how many people live in the home, criminal records and the list goes on. Unnecessary exposure. Most of us private citizens did not ask for any of this online advertisement. We have gone too far, I tell you! Too far!

In Dominica, people prefer to keep their private lives private, although this is hard to do with so many busybodies and nosy neighbors constantly prying and peeking into each others' business. In Dominica, unlike most places in the United states, doors are kept unlocked, many times, people will frequently invite themselves into your home. Forget calling first. They just show up and expect you to engage them in conversation no matter whether you are in the middle of cooking, laundry, or any state of undress. They will remain uninvited with absolutely no qualms about it. Yet, they do not want their personal failings broadcasted on the streets or airways. Their neighbors? Yes! But not theirs. No Way!

Chapter Three

Influence of Culture on Employment

Many immigrants to the United States, including myself, moved here without any other relatives close by. Those individuals who moved to the US to join family, eventually branched out on their own to start their family (spouse and children). Amid all of the distractions and attractions it can be a very lonely life. It would be nice to call a relative over or pop over to their house for a visit. In Dominica if you need an item or service, a friend or family member will be glad to come over to assist free of charge. Here, if you don't have it, unless you have a close friend nearby, you have to do without or go buy it. It seems like nothing is free in this country! Therefore, there is an added responsibility and burden to the new immigrant who does not have an established friend base. In the back of these independent-thinking individuals' minds is the desire to work hard and save. It is well-known that most families in the US are a few paychecks away from the poverty line or being homeless. No family member will take you and your children in because they are hundreds of miles away in another country. Yet, that will not keep us down for too long. Ambition, drive and hard work was instilled in myself and other Dominicans from an early age. So we maintain our cool, stay focused, set our goals and work hard to attain them.

Careers and Opportunities Are Different

Each person in society develops some values or personal worldview, some of which he or she obtained from his or her family. Environmental factors such as family, culture, and even the media play a central role in an individual's career choices as well. As a person becomes more exposed to these sources, their values, including work ethic become more important.

The opportunities for career advancement in most fields are limited on the island of Dominica, West Indies. So, people tend to remain in their occupations for many years, some for their entire working life without much expectation or actual promotions. During my childhood days and before, the most successful and wealthy people on the island were large landowners, entrepreneurs, and highly educated career people. My paternal grandfather was a landowner and fisherman, who owned his own boat, nets, and other fishing supplies. Similarly, my maternal grandfather was a landowner and property manager. Both my grandmothers were homemakers and seamstresses. During that generation, people wore several hats in order to provide for their families and build a foundation for their future. They also passed on their skills, beliefs, and values down to their children. This explains why my father is a landowner (one of the largest on the island today) and was fisherman and my mother was a seamstress and homemaker. In the Dominican culture, the fathers expected their children, especially their sons, to stay in the family business and preserve their family tradition. Today, these ideals may not be as pronounced or evident but the roots remain. Parents feel a sense of pride when their children show genuine interest in the family business enough to join with the parents and give it 100% of their effort.

Neither my grandparents nor parents completed elementary school. However, they emphasized the importance of an education and formal or advanced training for their children, particularly the girls. My father often said that he wanted his girls to be financially and intellectually independent, so they would not have to totally depend on any man for support. Ironically, in my father's generation and before, the men dominated their women. They controlled every aspect of their lives, including the number of children they would have and how they ran the household. I think that my father wanted his daughters to be free of the restraints that the men of his and former generations had placed on their women.

My earliest exposure to work was farm labor. I worked on the different family farms after school, on weekends and holidays. My siblings and I fed the animals, watered the plants, and harvested the crops. And on Saturdays, I accompanied my parents and other siblings to the local market to sell the produce. Back then, I did not like tough, manual labor. I still don't! I also did not like to sit in the marketplace waiting for customers who would often argue with me about the price, quality and quantity of the produce. Did I contend (pun intended) earlier that Dominicans love to argue? Regardless of your age they will take you on.

Before the tender age of eleven, I was a hard worker but could not always prove it because of my small physical size and limited physical strength. I was often teased by others for being too thin and weak. This experience surely did not increase my love for farm-work. Regardless of my disdain for this type of work, because I lived under my parents' roof, I had no choice but to do their bidding until I graduated from secondary school. I am sure if you were to ask other Dominicans (around my age group or older) they would share similar experiences with you.

After graduating with a Bachelor's degree in psychology from Florida International University, I took a position as an Early Interventions Officer in Fort Lauderdale, Florida. In this capacity, I assisted parents of children from birth to three years of age with various developmental delays in finding necessary care. For example, if a child needed speech therapy and physical therapy, I would facilitate and coordinate the care between the parent and child, and the provider. During that time, I began to seriously evaluate my career and educational options. I really was not sure what career I wanted to pursue, but I knew that I wanted it to be in one of the many fields of psychology, maybe: Social or Industrial and Organizational Psychology. I incorporated my beliefs and abilities in deciding my career path. After much prayer and consideration, I decided on a career in Professional Christian Counseling.

Culture, Sex, and Socioeconomics

In the US culture, sex, and socioeconomic status influence opportunities and social interactions amongst various groups. In the United States, Unfortunately, ethnic minorities are over-represented in low-income employment. Some issues that correlate to this statistics are discrimination and stereotypes against these groups. Another factor that impacts these groups is the limited choices access to role models/ positive influences. Some minorities such as Black/African-American may lack the confidence in their ability to succeed in their career of choice. Therefore, kids drop out of school at higher rates than their Caucasian counterparts.

In the past, generally there were separate sets of values for men and women, in Dominican society. Each gender has certain roles they could choose from. People from the older generations disapprove of women pursuing certain careers. For example, a woman being an architect or construction worker, or a man being a nurse were not widely practiced or accepted. People in my culture esteem careers like work in medicine, law enforcement, and political fields much higher than they do teaching and homemaking. All these beliefs and views impact my view of my roles and purpose in life. However, I refuse to allow them to limit my potential. Growing up, I was willing to accept the limitations of my circumstances, but I still dreamed of traveling abroad to Europe or the United States, Australia or another developed country to develop my interests and return home to begin and establish my career. I did not have any counseling role models while growing up. I had just heard and read about psychologists and counselors, but I did not meet one until I started college. I cannot help but feel that if I had spent some time interviewing a counselor or someone working in one of my areas of interest, maybe my path to choosing a career in professional counseling would have been much easier. However, I choose not to stay there and wallow in what could have been. I am truly thankful for who I am today. I am also truly thankful for where I am today!

Making choices that coincide with values are essential to satisfaction since values are core beliefs that people use to judge their performance and that of others. For a job to be satisfying, people need to believe that their daily tasks on the job are worthwhile. Behavior that contradicts an individual's values may hamper his or her decision-making abilities. In my case, I was not used to environments where supervisors and coworkers freely used obscene language on the job. These issues bothered me so much that I would later leave the employment because of the lack of professionalism found at the workplace.

In retrospect, I realize that I was experiencing "culture shock." I did not expect these attitudes, and clearly I did not know how to cope effectively with them on the job. I also terminated different employments because I knew that there were more and maybe better opportunities available for me. I could not justify being in those environments, although it helped pay our bills. I was dissatisfied and confused as to why employers allowed this behavior, so my best option was to sever ties with the company. Being young and idealistic you may say. It was the best way I knew of handling the situation back then.

The beliefs that someone has about himself or herself influence the way they approach life, including their career choices. If they do not have these strong beliefs or convictions, they will have problems with choosing careers and making other important decisions. Also, these individuals can be easily persuaded by different points of views. What confusion! People need to know what they are willing to do and why. People need to be ready to make strong arguments in support of their beliefs to employers, friends, or anyone else. I think there is less ambiguity in my life because I have core values that I am not willing to compromise. Further, I take pride in taking responsibility for and believing in something larger than myself, particularly something that has stood the test of time and has proven its worth. The foundation for my beliefs and attitudes is God and His Word. I strive to always embrace His *truth about me*. Regardless of attitudes, beliefs or overall negativity that others may try to spew out into my life.

Influence of Culture on Employment and the Workplace

It is extremely challenging for parents, Mainly moms who work outside the home. The day generally begins early and ends late. If meetings or tasks at work run late kids have to stay longer in aftercare or the parent may ask a friend or relative to pick them up. For families with grandmothers or grandfathers who care about their grandkids living nearby, it is a great relief and benefit to them. Grandparents love to see and be there for their grandchildren, and the grandchildren love going to their grams or grandpas. It is a win-win situation for all! Parents go to work, earn an income with peace of mind; whilst grandparents get to spend time with their grandbabies.

As a child in Dominica, I clearly remember most school-aged children had aunts, grandparents, or other family member, or even a neighbor in some instances that they could go to after school if their parents were not available. Most mothers were home with their children while they helped on their farm or did other types of work nearby. Today, for those families who do not have that kind of invaluable assistance, life can be a little more hectic. Children will get ill from time to time where they cannot go to childcare, school, or someone else's house. They have to stay home with their parent or guardian. Parents want to be reliable and keep their jobs but they have to take care of their child first. This is a scenario played out daily in so many families but never gets easier. Today, to help alleviate the tremendous distress and potential loss of employment, parents are finding creative ways of surviving. They work from home, or split time between the office and work at home.

If you are a single parent, you know you want a good paying job or career, which comes with long hours and sometimes travel. You need someone you can trust with your children and is willing to take them when you have to go out of town. Providing for the family is a must. As such, you have to make those choices and pray that it will all work out for the best. As mom, you can be a full-time student. You may have to spend all day at work, pick the kids up from school or childcare, prepare dinner, get them to bed, prepare for next day, then drive to your evening class at your local college or university some time during that same day. "What was that? Yes, I know, reading this long sentence got me breathless too!". That is the reality of many twenty-first century families. Fortunately, this part of life is just that one segment which only lasts for a season. Circumstances change for the better. Children do grow up and become more independent, requiring less one-on-one supervision. So hang in there if you are in this season of life. Keep your head up and keep moving forward . . .

Chapter Four

It Is So Hard to Find a True Friend

I hope I am not the only person asking, "Why is it so hard to make and keep true friends?" As a young child all they way up past my teenage years, I never had a lack of friends neither did I have a hard time making friends. At that particular stage of in my life, making and keeping close friends was second nature, to me. O, the sweet simplicity of childhood. Today, I still do not have a problem doing so. The major problem, though, is keeping trustworthy, dependable friends. Sometimes, people come into your life temporarily—for a short term. As humans made in the image of God we all desire relationships with others. We desire to share our lives with friends and loved ones.

Some friends seem like they are a great match and they blend in well with your family, beliefs, and total lifestyle. At first, you get to know each other and find that they are hot and cold, wishy-washy, undependable and unreliable. A huge disappointment! When you find friends who are around your age group, have kids around the same age as you, and hang out at the same places as your family, you would think that you would be friends for a long time. In other instances, you experience another major setback when you do find a genuine friend that you gel with and she moves to a different state or country. Then you maintain a long-distance friendship, not ideal at all. Not only do you need to "replace" this adult friend, you also need to find new friends and play-mates for your children as well.

Friend or Faux?

I have met many kinds of friends in my life thus far. The following paragraphs will describe the types of "friends" that I have encountered on my journey. The first type of friends I have come across are a bit *cagey*, to say the least. Actually, I am not sure if I can call them friends. I have concluded that some of the characteristic they exhibit are incongruent with lasting friendships. These are the same individuals who promise that they will be there for you. However, when that time comes when you truly need their support they are found wanting. They remain aloof and unconcerned. They will not buy the products or services that they had once promised to purchase from you. Nevertheless, with no hesitation they will tell you, "If you need anything, let me know. I am here for you." They are "no shows" when it comes to support for yourself or children.

There are people who are the "jealous type", who may also call themselves friends. They are envious and will compete with you even when you have no desire to do likewise. Sometimes, women tend to think that if another woman is attractive, then she is stuck-up or probably some sort of threat. I am not denying that some physically attractive women have those tendencies, but again you do not paint everyone with the same weak brush containing your own insecurity. We all have our weaknesses and shortcomings but to project that unto someone else will not benefit anyone. It is surprising but true, that those women with similar struggles prefer to bring each other down instead of working together to cope with their daily challenges.

I have also run across the "unreliable type" on my quest to find true friends. People have cell phones and house phones. In this high tech fast-paced world, they also have email and text messaging capabilities. Yet even with all this instant technology, they will tell you, "I didn't get your message." This excuse is completely untrue and holds no water. Another excuse I have heard is: "I was too busy to get back to your call or text." You didn't have a minute to send a text or e-mail, seriously? It is bad enough to say, "I forgot," but at least be honest about it. That friend doesn't want to be bothered and prefer to lie about it. The truth may hurt or sting a bit but the truth is the truth, which is all I ask. Friends are honest with each other. I have learned that in spite of it all that God's grace is sufficient for me, just like it was for the apostle Paul (2 Cor. 12:9). When friends are not there or are few and far between, the Lord will never leave or forsake me.

As human beings, we have to learn to accept our failures. We should be real with each other. I have tried every day to stop seeking approval from other people. It does not mean that I do not care what people say or think of me. Rather, it means that I will no longer allow others' approval to define me. When we hide failures, sooner or later they will come out. Then the shame will be compounded when people find out what we have been trying to hide for so long. Do not flaunt your problems. However, to have and keep good friends, we need to stop the fake airs and be real. We all have insecurities and failures but we know that only God can fill that need for approval and acceptance. Even Christ was tempted in every way. He gives us the strength to overcome these tendencies of focusing on other flawed human beings as our indicator of who we are, where we came from and where we are going in this life.

In Dominica, your friends would be yours for life, barring any major conflicts or death. Here, in America, people move so frequently that you may not have a lifelong friend in your local area. It is even harder when you are *the new kid, or new mom on the block* in the small group or women's Bible study group. Long distance friendships are better than none at all. However, due to the distance, the friends realize that the friendship is very different. Hence, necessary adjustments need to be made if the friendship is to survive and thrive. Good friends will be there at all times no matter what. This is the friendship I find lacking in my life and circle, currently. I am not saying I have no close friends but they are very few. I tend to believe that is the way it needs to be for now.

I have heard other women share similar stories. That is why I submit to you that it is high time that as women we find ways to put petty differences aside and support each other as mothers, sisters, daughters, and wives. If we can be there for each other and build each other up, I say, why not? I still believe there are good, solid friends out there for like-minded people. If you want to have friends, then you need to be a friend. One of my favorite verses is Proverbs 17:17: "A friend loves at all times . . ." This is the kind of friend that I want to be and the kind of friends I would love to have for a lifetime.

Chapter Five

Do Not Offend

People will curse openly in the United States, on the streets at work, almost anywhere. Some individuals in Dominica will practice this same disrespectful speech habits. I remember in my childhood days (during the 80's and early 90's) these same loose-lipped offenders would generally refrain from cursing in the presence of an authority figure like the police or teacher. Swearing was shunned, and you can get arrested for swearing in public. Even performers like rappers are censored and are prohibited from swearing on stage when performing on the island. If they do they will get fined by the authorities. It is evident after several trips back to Dominica and from reports circulating this behavior is becoming more and more acceptable. The acceptance of profanity as part of general conversation and dialogue can be explained as another distasteful trend found in so many other countries around the globe. No matter the consequences there are some people who definitely have no filter. They will say whatever, whenever to almost whomever. They do not care who is around and have no tact when they talk to others and about others. They just do not care. The word "sensitivity" doesn't exist in their vocabulary.

Child's Play

You remember the days when your parents told you to go play outside and you not to come back in until the sun went down? During the summer vacation, you played in the river and ocean all day and soaked in the water and the sun. There was no sunscreen and no parental supervision. An older brother, sister, or friend would suffice. This was the norm back then, not the exception.

For me, more often than not, we played with crude, homemade toys. We also played on rough concrete surfaces, gravel, or mud. We bumped all ten toes, scraped knees, fell down, got up, and kept on moving. We didn't just run to Momma for quick relief; we kept playing if it was not too bad. Then when we got home, our mom would apply some herbal medicine, or any other local medicine such as mercurochrome found in the house. Whatever happened to mercurochrome anyway? I just miss that red solution which seemed to heal any cut or bruise in quick time. It is quite alright to take a break and laugh at this juncture. We were up and about in no time with this care.

Today, some parents cringe if their kids play outdoors, or play contact sports such as football. Even boys are softer than girls. They are not at all as tough as the ones I grew up with and around. Children seem to have lost some of their competitive edge because they are told *everyone is a winner.* So this conclusion begs the question, *"why should they try to win?"* Playgrounds are padded and covered in mulch to prevent injuries. Don't get me wrong these are all great for our children's safety. However, the downside is that kids run to the moms for the smallest scratches and scrapes. Sometimes a scrape is just a scrape and doesn't warrant a trip to the emergency room. Being over-protective is harming instead of helping our children.

Another sore development is some responsible adults are afraid to correct or even talk to another child when they are doing something wrong because the parents might be offended. Parents are not thrilled when other parents or adults reprimand their children. These same parents may even be tempted to call the police if you look too hard when that child is behaving badly and disrupting other children and the people around.

Expectations of Children

One of the main cultural influences inherent in my background was my parents, expected their children to respect their elders. Also, people generally greeted each other with "good afternoon" or "good morning" or "good night" in any public setting. It doesn't matter if you know the person or not, the polite thing to do is to greet him or her. Remember, when people on the island say "goodnight," they mean hello, not good-bye like it means here in the United States. Even today, in Dominica children are still expected to demonstrate good manners.

In the United States, people will greet you with, "How are you?" without expecting an answer. When someone asked me, "How are you?" the first few times, I responded, "Very well, thank you. And you?" The response I got was a brief smile and quick nod. Later, I learned that I had to greet people the same way, "How are you?" not caring to hear how they were really doing. After living for almost two decades in America, ironically, I have become part of something that I found strange in the first place. I sometimes respond with, "How are you?"

In Dominica, children are not allowed to, and if they are, they will most likely be reprimanded for calling adults, especially the elderly, by their first names. Contrast this to the United States where children habitually call adults even their stepparents by their first names. Even some college professors want students to call them by their first name. All teachers are called Ms., by their "first name," or by their last names. Respect is the order of the day. Greetings like "yes, ma'am, no ma'am," "yes, sir," and "yes, Dad" are the norm, not an oddity. Additionally, children were not part of grown-up conversations. They would go outside or make themselves scarce while adults spoke. Kids could not interject and be part of the dialogue. It was a good practice because children, of course, should not be exposed to adult issues, if at all possible. Those standards are shifting today because on a recent visit, on different occasions, I noticed children and adults were all part of the conversations of mature content.

To put it simply, children run the homes. Discipline is optional in many US households. There are many styles and ways of raising kids. Furthermore, children have seemingly unlimited choices of toys, clothes, books, entertainment, and food. Options are everywhere for children. They do not have to do any household chores to gain any of these privileges. It is just part of their lives. They expect it all and the day these luxuries are not available, believe me, it is not a happy day for the parents who have overly indulged their little princes and princesses.

Devoting much of your time and energy to your children is commendable. However, the extreme that I observed over and over again is almost laughable if it was not so pathetic, in my view. Mothers get together and spend hours talking about their two and a half year olds' abilities and how advanced little Johnnie is. He can even do long division in his sleep. I can see their need for people to say, "You are such a great mom" or "You come from an amazing gene pool." I am not sure where it all comes from, or if they know that they are being ridiculous. These moms are actually competing with each other through their children. Yes, more cattiness and competition. Most definitely, I talk about my girls. Every good mom or dad does. However, the point I want the drive home here is that my children and their sweet little adventures 'do not" dominate my every conversation. I try to maintain a balance and talk about other life concerns, joys and pains. On more than one play date, I have *spied with my own little eyes* moms talking to other moms, and focusing on their little tyke while ignoring other little ones. They will not even encourage their son or daughter to share toys with the other children present. It is a play date after all. One of the goals is for our children to develop social skills. Surely, this one child is not the star of the show. They do not want their child to experience any discomfort whatsoever. It is especially pronounced with mothers who have only one child. They don't realize that the world does not revolve around their child, who no doubt knows his multiplication tables and does algebra all before he turns three. It is OK to let a child amaze and entertain you in his or her own childlike way. However, let us be adults here. Allow others and yourself to talk about more than just our children when we get together. For instance we can talk about: how to be a gracious hostess, or be able to hold a meaningful conversation for more than five minutes, or pay attention to other kids, act like you care, and not just focus the spotlight on your child. I have seen it too many times to be surprised anymore, but it is no less disturbing.

Do I Really Offend You?

Today, in the United States, the national anthem, "The Star-Spangled Banner" offends some individuals because it is too violent. I am not making this up. Some people really think that way. They claim it focuses too much on war and bloodshed. Do they not know the history of the United States and all the wars that were fought to guarantee all these freedoms.

Oh, say can you see by the dawn's early light
What so proudly we hailed at the twilight's last gleaming
Whose broad stripes and bright stars thru the perilous fight,
O'er the ramparts we watched were so gallantly streaming?
And the rocket's red glare, the bombs bursting in air,
Gave proof through the night that our flag was still there.
Oh, say does that star-spangled banner yet wave
O'er the land of the free and the home of the brave.

Today, are we becoming more ignorant, wimpy, or both? We all went to preschool or elementary school and remember some of the nursery rhymes and songs they taught us. These rhymes were tragic, miserable, violent, silly, and in many cases made absolutely no sense at all. I am not sure what was going through the minds of these poets, but looking back, they sure were fun to sing and dance to. If these writers and composers were still alive today, these activists would give them non-stop grief and attempt to sue them for mental distress. Do you remember these classics?

- ❖ Humpty Dumpty sat on a wall. Humpty Dumpty had a great fall. All the king's horses and all the king's men couldn't put Humpty together again.

- ❖ Jack and Jill went up the hill to fetch a pail of water
  Jack fell down and broke his crown and Jill came tumbling after.
  Up Jack got and home did trot,
  As fast as he could caper;
  And went to bed and bound his head
  With vinegar and brown paper
  Then Jill came in, and she did grin,
  To see Jack's paper plaster;
  Her mother whipped her, across her knee,
  For laughing at Jack's disaster.

- ❖ My Bonnie lies over the ocean,
  My Bonnie lies over the sea,
  My Bonnie lies over the ocean,
  O bring back my Bonnie to me.

- ❖ Georgie Porgie, pudding and pie,
  Kissed the girls and made them cry
  When the boys came out to play
  Georgie Porgie ran away.

❖ Rock-a-bye, baby, in the tree top
  When the wind blows the cradle will rock
  When the bough breaks the cradle will fall
  Down will come baby, cradle and all

❖ Little Miss Muffet sat on a tuffet
  Eating her curds and whey,
  Along came a spider,
  Who sat down beside her
  And frightened Miss Muffet away.

❖ Ring around the rosy (Ring-a-ring o' rosies)
  A pocket full of posies
  "Ashes, ashes" ("A-tishool! A-tishoo!")
  We all fall down

❖ London Bridge is falling down,
  Falling down, falling down,
  London Bridge is falling down,
  My fair lady.

❖ In a cavern, in a canyon,
  Excavating for a mine
  Dwelt a miner forty niner,
  And his darling Clementine.
  Oh my darling, oh my darling,
  Oh my darling, Clementine!
  Thou art lost and gone forever
  Dreadful sorry, Clementine.
  Light she was and like a fairy,
  And her shoes were number nine,
  Herring boxes, without topses,
  Sandals were for Clementine.
  Drove she ducklings to the water
  Ev'ry morning just at nine,
  Hit her foot against a splinter,
  Fell into the foaming brine.
  Ruby lips above the water,
  Blowing bubbles, soft and fine,
  But, alas, I was no swimmer,
  So I lost my Clementine.
  How I missed her! How I missed her,

How I missed my Clementine,
But I kissed her little sister,
I forgot my Clementine.

❖ Jack Sprat could eat no fat His wife could eat no lean
And so betwixt the two of them
They licked the platter clean
Jack ate all the lean, Joan ate all the fat.
The bone they picked it clean, Then gave it to the cat
Jack Sprat was wheeling, His wife by the ditch. The barrow turned over,
And in she did pitch. Says Jack, "She'll be drowned!" But Joan did reply,
"I don't think I shall, For the ditch is quite dry."

❖ There was an old woman who lived in a shoe
She had so many children, she didn't know what to do;
She gave them some broth without any bread;
Then whipped them all soundly and put them to bed.

❖ Peter Piper pumpkin-eater,
Had a wife and couldn't keep her;
He put her in a pumpkin shell,
And there he kept her very well.

❖ John Jacob Jingleheimer Schmidt,
His name is my name too.
Whenever we go out,
The people always shout,
There goes John Jacob Jingleheimer Schmidt.
Dah dah dah dah, dah dah dah

❖ Mother, may I go out to swim?
Yes, my darling daughter,
Hang your clothes on a hickory limb,
But don't go near the water.
You may look cute in your bathing suit,
But act just as you oughter,
Now and then you can flirt with the men,
But don't go near the water.

The list of songs and rhymes go on and on . . . Think about the lyrics of those songs. Some of these nursery rhymes do contain adult themes. woven throughout. Even the fairytales about Beauty and the Beast, Sleeping Beauty, Snow-white and the Seven Dwarfs had some tragedy and scary elements in there as well. Obviously, as children we didn't take the time to ponder on the words or meanings too much. We were too busy making sure we know these stories, and sang the songs at the top of our lungs. We had fun. As far as I know, these songs did not lead to me being traumatized or growing up to be depressed or a violent, law-breaking individual. Even my conservative parents never said, "Stop singing that Humpty Dumpty song. It is too violent and against what we stand for in this home!" It didn't happen. It doesn't mean that because you disagree with something, someone else should be banned from practicing or saying it. All of this politically correct (PC) stuff cripples creativity and personal growth. Where is the fun in life people? Where?

Contradictions

America is an individualist rather than a collectivist society like, say, China. People strive for personal success. They love to work on themselves and for themselves. Nothing wrong with the idea of individualism, but there is still a fine balance that one needs to maintain. We have to be there for each other. We are responsible for our behavior. True. Notwithstanding, I emphasize "no man is an island" is still true today. Amongst all this rugged individuality lies several pronounced contradictions. Take a look at these examples:

+ People need and love privacy, but they will go on television shows or news or reality shows given the slightest chance. They will jump at their fifteen minutes of fame and gobble up every distasteful, indigestible moment of it. People will be caught up in scandal and all kinds of off-the-wall behavior and will be laughed at or blamed, but a few months later, the public will embrace them openly. The public is generally forgiving and has a limited memory. Many of these disgraced people will even gain a radio or television show after their high fall from grace. They will go on Springer or Wendy and talk about the most intimate details of their lives on national television. They will air family disputes on television as well. Hence the popularity of the shows of Judge Judy, Judge Joe Brown, Judge Mathis, and People's Court. Yet these very same people will think nothing of building a ten-foot privacy fence to keep nosey neighbors out. Only in America!

- People are individualistic, yet many neighborhoods or subdivisions have a Home Owners' Association (HOA). Even though you may not want to, you must join the HOA, and you are expected to pay the fees if you live in certain neighborhood. Thus, with your hard earned money you take care of the community, the pool, the tennis courts, and the sidewalks. However, in these neighborhoods people walk or drive to their home and don't have anything much to say to each other until the next HOA meeting.

- Great rule: "Kids do not talk to strangers." Yet kids will go from door to door to collect candy from neighbors and total strangers at Halloween. Yes, it is a tradition to some, but I cannot yet grasp any benefit of Halloween. Do our kids really need more candy and chocolate? Have the parents/guardians checked the obesity stats on young children lately?

- People feel that they are free to be creative and accept themselves with all their imperfections. Yet they will have plastic/cosmetic surgery on their faces and all other parts of their anatomy. Maybe I am missing the point here. It could just be that the mere act of having plastic surgery is being truly creative.

- People will declare their undying love for their parents and grandparents but will send them to a nursing home in a heartbeat rather than keeping them at home. Who needs the extra stress?! It is a ton of work, true enough. However, the idea that many individuals place a higher value on maintaining their youthful looks over taking care of their elderly parent is a bit disconcerting to say the least. People will lie about their age and do everything to make themselves appear to be younger than their true age, yet claim to love the elderly. They even brag about how they want to age gracefully. I say, "To each his own."

Every society and culture has its traditions and contradictions. The key is to learn to embrace the positive traits and facets, and eradicate the negative and toxic ones.

Chapter Six

Mannerisms and Behavior

I firmly believe we should make a conscious effort to learn about the history and norms of the country that we live in. I am still learning so much and still have a lot to learn about the history and life in the United States. When you did not go to elementary school or high school in a country, unless you had in-depth studies on that country in your homeland your knowledge would be very limited. Furthermore, misinformation and misconceptions are part of this knowledgebase. The information you got was from school, the news, books, and maybe family and friends who traveled to that country were skewed one way or another. Therefore, you may feel ill-equipped to talk intelligently about your new home.

So many things that you see—like a confederate flag or a bald eagle— have no significance to you until you find out the roots of the object or symbol. Even certain parks, the location of the town you go to innocently for business or entertainment only to find out that slaves were lynched there or the mob once ruled this part of town. Every place has its history; you can appreciate or respect it only when you know about it. As a visitor or a foreigner, it is automatic to make assumptions based on your experiences or stories you may have heard from locals or other visitors. However, when you learn about the real history, your perspective, attitude, and behaviors toward that object, event, or place will change.

Basic Mannerisms

This section may sound critical but it is not meant to be negative. It is reality. Read on. There are clear differences between the way people in Dominica and people in US interact. For example, back in Dominica, there is no strong expectation to maintain constant eye contact when having a conversation with another person. You may feel more comfortable looking away and then making eye contact from time to time. Here, if you do not look someone in the face when talking to them, you might come across to others as disrespectful, uninterested, or even untrustworthy. In the Dominican culture, we do not use hand gestures when carrying on a conversation, as much as I see in the United States. As a matter of fact someone can give a two hour speech with their hands hanging limply at their side. When excessive hand gesturing is used when speaking, the onlookers say that the speaker is a 'boaster" "dramatic" or "showing off." In Dominica, people look at each other's facial expressions to gauge emotions. People talk more with their facial expressions than their hands.

Dominicans on the whole are very assertive and sometimes verbally and physically aggressive. They speak their minds and are not intimidated or afraid of offending others. People have no problems eavesdropping on your conversations and jumping in and giving their advice without so much as an "excuse me." Yes, they are friendly, but I find it off-putting and rude when people take over your conversation without an invitation. People stare you down when you walk down the street and will act like they know you, personally. They will not look away. If they want to look they will. They will talk to you with marked disdain in their voice if you ignore these unwanted advances (especially from the men) *Unreal.* We called these characters "boldface" back in the day.

Parents expect both boys and girls to stand up for themselves and engage in verbal and physical fights when necessary. I have since maintained some of these values and rejected others. I do not like offending others. Furthermore, I prefer to encourage others rather than confronting them. Once again, my personality and beliefs have influenced my decisions to either accept or reject cultural norms no matter where I may be on this earth.

Dominicans have always been active people. They walked to the stores. Young people play soccer, cricket and other sports regularly. They did not spend as much time driving on the highway, this may be one reason why Dominicans had fewer problems with obesity and heart diseases. Sadly, this has changed to a great extent to reflect much of

Western society. Too many residents now are obese and prefer to be immobile rather than active. I hope they revert to the original ideals for health, wellness and fitness soon because the harmful effects of lack of physical activity and consumption of unhealthy foods is too much for the Nature Isle to handle. It will all lead to heartache and other tragic consequences.

When you return to your homeland after living abroad for several years, your attitudes and mannerisms would be different to a certain extent. It should be no surprise when the locals call you "Americanized" or an American since they cannot relate to the differences they see in you. Many times, they believe that it is intentional even when it is not. You may tell a family member, "I am hot; therefore I cannot wear this jacket and stockings." They will respond in disgust, "You were born here, so what are you complaining about?" when in fact, you were not complaining. You were just expressing how you felt at that time. Sadly, some of the same people who are so critical are also envious because they wish that they would be the one returning to America and not you. Many of them would sell their soul to respond to the invitation written by Emma Lazarus, which is now engraved on the plaque at the Statue of Liberty: "Send me your poor, tired, huddled masses yearning to be free." My friends I assure you there is absolutely no need for envy. You can live a full life wherever in the world you may be at this time.

On the Island of Dominica, at social settings, people will talk and argue about Anything. They do not use vulgar or crude language, in most instances. But they will express their thoughts and feelings nonetheless. On the other hand, in the United States, most people have this unwritten rule not to talk about certain topics. Some of these topics include the following:

- Politics
- Religion
- Income
- And in some cases the cost of homes and items

However, in Dominica, these topics are all fair game, and people actually look forward to discussing them. People often believe that they can ask you any question and expect a direct, honest answer. They will not even blink when they ask. Personal or not, a large percentage of native Dominicans think it is their right to know. Moreover, it is your obligation to share. Sheeesh, seriously, that is my private affair and I choose to keep it that way.

Pets

People treat pets as children, sometimes even better than children in the United States. They dress them up and carry them around in their arms. Pets eat from special china at the dinner table. They even sleep in their owners' beds and ride in their front seats of their vehicles. Pets are part of the family. In my culture, pets are just that—pets. Big dogs will generally be used as guard dogs. Dogs, especially, may come indoors but sleep in their outside house/kennel. They do not receive any of that aforementioned attention. Dominicans see their pets as animals, not as half human. They treat them well but keep them in their rightful place instead of elevating them to human status.

Church

People can be very casual when they attend church services in the United States. They wear shorts, jeans, T-shirts, spaghetti strap dresses, flip-flops, and backs out. In certain churches, you stand out if you are dressed up. In the Caribbean, people wear their Sunday best—beautiful dress, stockings, high heels, suit and jackets for the men with dress shoes, not sneakers. Little girls wear socks and shoes with long frilly, colorful dresses. You wonder how people could wear so many warm clothes when it is so hot and balmy outside. They do so because they are used to it. This is the tradition. It's always been that way for most churchgoers. Going "to church" requires dress up in ones very best. If I go back to the island to church today without stockings and wear short sleeves, churchgoers will undoubtedly stare at me. They will look at me and do an obvious double take. Some bold folks may have the audacity to even ask me, "Why are you wearing this and not that?" I will simply respond, "Because I choose to." Furthermore can't you feel the heat?" They will look at me in disdain like I have completely lost my mind. Many Caribbean people who have lived on the islands all their lives do not understand life outside their little home country. Thus, they also find it very difficult to adapt to change or anything that is different.

Adults and children attend the same services in Dominica. Children attend Sunday School but are expected to sit with the mature audience and discuss mature subject matters at any age. The preachers believe that as long as it is in the Bible, it should not be censored. Any age should hear it and not be affected by it negatively. It is fine for the preacher to discuss these subjects in the church which takes the responsibility off the shoulder of the parents. After all, it is the Word of God. Not thinking for an instant that the word has a time and place and audience, based on the matters discussed or presented in a sermon. The pulpit was the place for teaching social studies, geography, biology, and some theology sprinkled in. It was the norm, not the exception, to hear messages from the Song of Solomon and other topics laced with sexual content during the Monday evening Bible study or another service during the week, no matter what age group was present. Maybe parents thought that if they sent their child to church, they would not have to worry about teaching them about the birds and the bees. What a mindset!

I cannot tell you how many times I heard long sermons and messages on topics dealing with adultery, fornication, murder, deceit, and other issues that I had no clue how to process or even comprehend. I would sit and blush internally with embarrassment, especially if I was sitting next to a boy around my age, all the while pretending like those mature topics did not faze me in the least. I would take a quick glance at the boy and he would look at me in a knowing and teasing kind of way, which embarrassed me even more. Those feelings while sitting during a church service were so pronounced during my teenage years that I often dreaded the message I would hear. I still remember many of these messages today, not fondly, I might add. A child should not have to endure any of this. However, talk to the preachers today, and they will tell you that was the only way to present the word to children at that time. Thankfully, in the United States, my children receive messages appropriate for their age level and are not introduced to certain subject matters. At this time, I cannot confirm whether the churches in Dominica have adopted the latter approach. But it is an idea which they should consider, in my book.

In Dominica as well as other Caribbean islands in the Protestant groups, when people pray, they will use 'thee,' 'thou,' and 'thine.' You may wonder, why are they still using King James English when they pray. The answer for many is that that is how they were brought up or trained. That is what they are used to, and they will keep on doing so. It also gives an air of importance and deeper spiritual understanding and closeness to the Word of God, some believe. Is anything wrong with praying that way? Certainly not! But to some other believers, it goes even deeper. They will contend, dogmatically, that it is irreverent or disrespectful to use "you" and "yours" when talking to God. The King James Version is the only acceptable way to pray even though you do not speak that way every day. Here is a thought: God the creator of *all* understands every language, even the other versions of English. And no, it is not disrespectful to pray to him in modern English. Using American English or any other language is just fine, and I am pretty sure the Most High God receives prayers from His children no matter what language they use.

Being On Time

If someone in Dominica tells you that they will meet you at 10:00 a.m., think more like 11:00 a.m. Timekeeping is not a big factor for island people. The radio programs or even live shows for different cultural events do not begin on time. They feel no need to rush. They will get there when they get there. They normally say around "ten" or "ten-ish." I got annoyed back then when I lived there when people were late, and I still get annoyed today. Generally, in the United States if you do not show up on time, you will be left behind. This attitude is more my speed (no pun intended).

Obsession with Sports Stars and Other Celebrities

During football, baseball or even basket ball seasons, in the US people paint their faces with the team colors. People can be mega fans who eventually turn to be stalkers. People tattoo the names of celebrities on their bodies. They wear team jerseys and pretend like they know the team members personally. They act like they know the movie stars. People get infatuated with the rich and famous. They will do anything to meet them and spend time with them. In Dominica, generally people admire celebrities and respect them, but they do not try to jump on them. They watch the game; have their favorite teams and players. They root for their team, enjoy the game and go home. These sports enthusiasts do not try to jump over security barricades to kiss these stars or athletes, or attempt to enter into their hotel rooms. They are just mere mortals with some fame and fortune, but still human, not God.

Crime

During my childhood days in Dominica, violent crimes were rare even though some of police officers did not carry guns, just batons. Serial murderers do not exist there. Does murder happen? Yes, but very infrequently. I felt safe walking the streets alone. Parents left their children home alone to run errands. Doors were still left unlocked while people are home. We even left them unlocked when we went out of the village or town. It is still very safe compared to the US or the other Caribbean islands. Returning Dominicans and first time visitors alike should feel quite comfortable walking or driving on Dominican highways and byways.

You don't believe me? That's quite alright. Go to Dominica and find out for yourself.

People with Disabilities

In America, the disabled are given equal rights and great treatment, ramps for their wheelchair scooters or other mobile devices. I remember during my childhood days that people with major disabilities were often shunned or looked down on. People who are mute, deaf, and blind were usually secluded and kept away from the general public. People felt uncomfortable around them; conversely, I am sure that people with disabilities felt uncomfortable around the "normal" people too. Even today people with certain physical impairments are referred to as that particular disability. For instance, "One Eye Larry" and "One arm Jack" would be used Instead of just "Larry or "Jack." I suspect this attitude might be common in other cultures and countries as well. Research this matter and find out for yourself. Most citizens felt pity for them but preferred not to deal with them. Fortunately, people are becoming more sensitive to the developmentally challenged and disabled every passing day in Dominica. In this country, thankfully they are given legitimate opportunities to work and live full lives to the extent they can. They become productive citizens who help and serve others. You can find them working at places like the supermarkets and restaurants. The developmentally challenged are quite often the most cheerful and helpful employees there.

Chapter Seven

Surviving a Down Economy

There are some practical things that are second nature to me. Many Americans may not be naturally inclined to reuse items. Discarding objects is an easier course of action will I dare say for the majority of American citizens. In Dominica, we reuse so many things—paper bags, grocery plastic bags, juice bottles, cans, and so on. We reuse them for water and other basic household needs. We hardly throw anything away unless it is completely useless. Dominicans know how to save, conserve and live with limited resources.

Recycle and Reuse

People in the United States throw away so much, even perfectly fine reusable plastic bowls. In Dominica and many of the other islands, people were green before *going green* was the new fad or buzz word. People who have struggled from the time that they were born understand how to save and survive in the worst of times. They keep moving forward and do not give up. They reuse products any way they can, *to make their money stretch.* They collect water in buckets from roof gutters. After carefully washing and disinfecting the containers, they also reuse plastic bottles and any other product that can be saved. Even when it is clearly labeled, "one-time use only," they will try to reuse it. We reuse plastic disposable plates, cups, and spoons, even foil paper. Dominicans know how to conserve when we do not have excess. Others have mentioned it to me and I have noticed it myself, even when Dominicans (including me) acquire more resources or material possessions we still fall back on using less and saving more, which is quite contrary to the mainstream American way of thinking. If you follow that philosophy, save more and use less during lean times, you are better able to survive without some of these luxuries, which were thought of as necessities. The US economy has been the top in the world for so long that people don't have a clue how to circumvent these tough times they currently face.

Practical Ideas that Work

In this down economy, people still want to maintain the same lifestyle with less income. It is not possible. If you want specific financial advice for your particular situation, consult a financial advisor, which I am not. You can listen on the radio or television to experts like Clark Howard and Dave Ramsey. These experts will be able to guide you accordingly. However, I do have some general practical suggestions that will be sure to work and alleviate your financial stresses and strains. Here we go:

- Make coupons your friend.
  Use them whenever you can. You can get them online in newspapers, from friends and other sources. Go get them.
- Buy generic products, instead of name brands, whenever possible Most times the ingredients are the same, or the product is the same quality so use them.
- Find your local goodwill and thrift stores.
  Certain products can be bought used and still have great value and effectiveness. Find what works best for you and your family.
- Visit consignment stores with a list and budget.
  Spend money only on things you need. You can also take in items to consign as well.
- Buy pre-owned, instead of new cars.
  The benefits of this one goes without saying. The new car depreciates in value more than the used one.
- Use cash or debit cards instead of credit cards.
  If you cannot pay for it unless is a complete necessity or investment like your house, do not buy it.
- Create a budget and stick to it.
- Change your mobile and home phone plans; change to more economic ones instead of the main and more popular companies.

- Eat out less and cook your own food at home.
  It is healthier and saves you money.
- Send your child's meal to school instead of buying food at school every day.
- Vacations may not be possible, so stay local and discover your state, and your kids will have fun (popularly known as staycation). It is not about the location; it is about the memories and the fact that you are together as a family.
- If you have to go on vacation, see if you can stay with a family member or see if you are able to rent a condo or house, which may be cheaper than a hotel
- Turn off all nonessential appliances before leaving your house.
- Buy energy-efficient appliances.
- Cancel cable or satellite TV, or get rid of some channels.
- Your child should choose one or two extracurricular activities, which will benefit the family. Do not enroll your child in so many activities and sports that your wallet is squeezed dry at the end of each month.
- Cut down on the number of times you drive to the grocery store in a week. Plan your trips and get the most possible done in one trip.
- Plan your days, and you will save time and energy and manage your days better
- Be creative: Take time to create a product or service that people may need or want. Extra income does not hurt.
- Take care of your landscaping/yard. Mow your lawn instead of paying a lawn/landscaping company to do so
- Shop at the Dollar Store: Many times, you will find similar products such as laundry detergent and dishwashing liquid of similar quality for one dollar. Look at it in figures $1.00.
- Finally, save, save, and save!

Chapter Eight

Many Cultures and Accents

The United States is a wonderfully complex country that comprises of several ethnicities and languages. Some people will argue that there are many races plus ethnicities. However, I contend that we are all the same (singular) race, called the "human race," with all kinds of variations. But I digress. People are placed into racial and ethnic categories whether they believe in them or not. We can discuss the reasons or necessity for such groups in another forum. Let me just inform my readers that I was not aware of many of these racial categories or emphasis on such categories before I arrived in the United States. I do not recall having to fill in ethnicity or race on any form in Dominica. So you can imagine my initial reaction to this direction: "Indicate Your Race."

Take a look at any form that you fill out daily, whether official or just a brief survey, and you will discover certain similarities. Because we fill out these forms so many times over we do not pay close attention to the type of information required at the top. At the doctor's office, school, church, employment, online applications, and the list goes on, you will find these questions. Here is a sample:

Please select one of the following:
Ethnic/Racial Origin (Select one)
___ White (not Hispanic origin)
___ Asian or Pacific Islander

___ Black (not Hispanic origin)
___ Hispanic/Latino (non-White)
___ Native American or Alaskan Native
___ Other
Marital Status: ___ Married ___ Single ___ Divorced ___ Separated
Gender: ___ Male ___ Female ___ Do not wish to answer

Draw your own conclusions, my dear reader. However, the reactions I have observed over time vary from one end of the spectrum to the next. Some people will answer the questions without a hint of annoyance. They will happily comply. Still, many people will argue that they fall into more than one category. Therefore, they will not fill in any of the information. Some individuals say they refuse to be categorized; some select "other." While some persons state that "other" makes them feel like an afterthought. Therefore, they l choose to leave this information blank.

Racism

This previous section provided a neat little segue onto the topic of racism. Yes, racism does exist. I never got followed in a store before I landed here. I was not aware of these negative attitudes until my friend pointed them out to me. I didn't get nasty looks for no reason other than I am not a Caucasian. I remember walking into certain stores (where store clerks were predominantly White) with my friend. I noticed that the clerks looked at us more closely just because of our skin color. Yes, it seems that only black people are shoplifters. Before, my friend's quick, abbreviated class on attitudes of Whites toward Blacks in certain settings, I was blissfully oblivious to this shopping dynamic.

Driving while black (DWB) is a well-known diagnosis. This term refers to the notion that Black people especially black men are habitually pulled over by the police for the smallest infraction, or none, except that they are Black. This should not be. Yet in a fallen world; it can be seen even in such a great country with so many open minds and arms and hearts. *Tolerance and acceptance* seems to be the buzz words of the day. Let's pray that the busy bees of political correctness in the wrong areas can redirect their energy and vast levels of influence to sting racism out!

Accents Galore

Where else in the world can you go to the library to find books, cds and dvds on almost any language Where else can you find language classes or teachers in your local area? It is amazing how many languages, including Chinese, Spanish, French, Vietnamese, Italian, Russian, German, Dutch, and the list goes on, are spoken in the United States—in local cities, towns, counties, and states! This is great! Naturally, with all these languages come various accents. You would expect people to be used to varying accents and manners of speech right? Wrong!

When I first arrived in the United Stares, people would announce to me I had a "thick accent." They would make comments like, "Your accent is so strong. Are you Jamaican?" I would reply, "No. I'm from Dominica" The automatic response would then be, "Oh, the Dominican Republic? So you speak Spanish." Then I would have to explain that I was from Dominica, an English-speaking island in the Eastern Caribbean. Then they would be even more confused since most of my audience had not heard of such an island. Then some would invariably say, "It is not Jamaica, but what is the difference? I thought all the islands were the same!" For those of my readers who know anything about the islands or even South America, people are very proud of their countries. They are patriotic to a fault. They see nationalism as something to be embraced. In the same way that people from Peru do not care to be classified as Hispanic, or Cubans or be called the same as Mexicans, Dominicans do not like to be called Jamaican, or vice versa. In the grand scheme of things, you will see that even though all these islands are so small and have more similarities than differences; people will take offence to being referred to as being from somewhere they are not. Personally, I was not offended, just miffed that the Americans who asked did not know the differences. I sometimes felt annoyed when I was asked over and over again, "where is Dominica again?" A word to the wise, people like to be referred to as being from: "where they are really from." Do not assume that they want to be affiliated with a neighboring island/country. Makes sense? If not, pause, breathe in and out twice, and let this concept sink in . . .

Accept and Embrace

Some people will accept and embrace you no matter what. Others will look at you with suspicion or look down on you if you are not from their culture or country. I hear all the time how visitors view Americans as arrogant, selfish, and individualist. Some Americans are those things in some cases. Still, they are caring and sensitive, overall.

I find myself from the beginning until today very uncomfortable, if not offended, when people refer to me as a minority or being from a *Third World Country*. On the surface, it is just unacceptable to me. These two terms or categories carry such negative connotations, feelings of inferiority, insignificance, and less than. Yes, I understand what they may mean by using those terms, but it doesn't matter. I still do not agree with them. I have mulled these incidents and different ideologies in my mind several times over. In the final analysis, I am still grateful to be here. This is the land for all. There is freedom and acceptance, but to me, these loaded words are anything but acceptable. I will remain open to making new friends and being friendly to all and never intentionally make anyone feel like they do not belong.

Pronounce What

People in different states have different accents. Furthermore, different regions of the country have similar accents. For instance, the southern states sound alike, and so do the northern states. Similarly, people in different villages and towns in Dominica have very distinct ways of speaking. You may refer to it a dialect, or even accent. Someone new to the island may not notice these nuances right away. At first, it was difficult to completely understand all the different accents and word pronunciations, in the US. I have noticed though that Americans sometimes do not bother to listen to what the speaker is saying. Rather, they focus on the accent and then say, "I can't understand what you are saying." Some Americans automatically assume that English is not your first language if you do not have a similar or familiar accent.

It is true, Dominicans do stress any syllable in the word. It doesn't matter as long as they pronounce the word. For instance, to pronounce the word metaphor. They will stress either the "me" or "ta" or "phore." There is no telling which syllable a Dominican will stress on in a word such as "adolescents." But I can tell you that there is not a single Dominican living in Dominica, who has heard a foreign accent that they did not like. They actually gravitate towards people with overseas accents. And you might hear them trying to sound like them not too long after. They will say about another Dominican National, "Hear so and so trying to yank. He thinks he is American too!" This is so hilarious! By and large, they do not make fun of a foreigner's accent or tell them with any disgust that they cannot understand them. Imitation is the way they cope and make the guest feel welcome. Imitation is truly the best form of flattery. Take it from me, Dominicans take the cake in that arena.

Grammar and Word Spelling

It is so funny that there is a British and American version for the same word with the same pronunciation. As a freshman in college, I had a difficult time remembering to change the word spellings from my original "British" English to the "American" version. I clearly remember my first paper in my composition. I got an A, but I had so many corrected spellings that it was unbelievable. For words like neighbor, I wrote neighbour; for savior, I wrote saviour; for check, I wrote cheque; behaviour for behavior; for mommy, mummy; for favor, favour; and the list goes on. Now, when I write to my family back home, I look at their spellings and just laugh and they do the same to mine. They also write the date differently: month, day, and then year. In the US, we write the date, and on most forms or official documents in this order: the day, month, and year. It can be confusing when they want to say April 6, 1989, and rewrite 6/4/1989, which I interpreted as June 4, 1989. You can see where the confusion can sink in, so before I send in any official documents, I always double check to err on the side of caution. A simple mistake could really set one back quite a bit depending on the type of document.

A quick lesson here is to take the time to know people as individuals and not lump them into nice neat categories. Often these categories DO NOT work, or are just plain useless and downright insulting to the individuals in question. Love, Live and Lift up!

Closing Remarks

Life Is Not So Different After All

I know we would appreciate life more if we saw it from the eyes of another and not just our narrow view. It is not that we can always do something about changing a new person or a stranger's situation. Instead, we can act in certain ways to make them feel comfortable and begin to adjust into their new setting. Yes, it may be that you are unfamiliar with their culture or way of thinking. It is all foreign to you. And it is true they came to this country hopefully to have a better life for themselves and their families. But take it from me; it is not an easy process. Remember you are also foreign to the foreigner. People are people no matter their circumstances or country of origin. If a decent person, or not even a decent person but someone who is working toward becoming a better human being reaches out to you, do not turn away. Make them feel welcome because you might be "entertaining an angel in disguise" (Hebrews 13:2). Imagine that. Would you want to miss out on the blessing that they may have brought into your life? As for me, I will be hospitable, generous, kind, and show compassion to as many people as possible.

The culture shock has worn off, but do I get homesick at times? For sure I do. People may not take the time to figure out why people shy away from certain groups or settings. It may be because they feel insecure around others, they feel they may be judged as well. If you are new to America or wherever you live, take the time to see yourself and others in the context of their culture before assuming that you are right and they are wrong. Your perception is not reality. In some instances, you will find that some things are just lost in translation. We are all different, yet we can all live together in one society if each one looks out first for the well-being of the other. The second greatest commandment will *never* change, "You shall love your neighbor as yourself" (Mark 12:3, NKJV). Take a moment and imagine what it would be like living one day as a person from a different cultural background from yours. How do they view you? Go ahead ask them.

I am still coming to terms with life and cultural experiences in a country other than my homeland. While I may never be comfortable with all that the United States has to offer, that could be true if I go anywhere in the world. The challenges will persist whether I return to Dominica or not. However, I am thankful to be where I am in life, at this moment. I am enjoying this season of life.

I often wonder what life would offer me, and what I would offer Dominica if I returned to live permanently in the land of my birth. Will I readjust? Will I feel at home? Will I function like the native that I am or will I experience culture shock and have great difficulty and be miserable? Sometimes, I think I need to return sooner rather than later. It would be great to have a simpler life where I grew up. I know my family would welcome me back. However, we will have to wait and see what the future holds for my family.

Yes, I am still amazed and often disturbed when people, including relatives, try to impose their views and beliefs on me. I am able to listen and see other's point of view most times, but I do not see how one adult can dictate to another adult what they should do and the choices they need to make. Let each adult live and thrive. Like it or not, they will make their own choices. My advice is: Do not allow anyone to dictate your worth, who you are, or who you will be. They do not have that power, so do not give it to them.

We should all appreciate that each culture and ethnicity, and country of origin not (not just our own) has a lot to offer the world. We should not be so narrow-minded, and believe in the superiority of our own ethnic group or culture otherwise known as "ethnocentricism," that we do not learn from others. We need to be seeking to enhance our experience in this life, which at the end of the day is so fleeting. We do not have to agree with every aspect of anyone's culture or personal life, but we should respect them anyway. The Latin proverb "E pluribus unum" meaning "Out of Many One" is a great motto to keep in mind as we continue on this life's journey. It was the motto suggested by the committee Congress appointed on July 4, 1776, to design "a seal for the United States of America." It is also carried by the American Eagle. I say, "Live and let live." "Do unto others as you would like others to do unto you." Be respectful of others. In the final analysis we are all mortals just passing through.

Acknowledgments

Firstly, I thank God for giving me the ability to share my experiences and thoughts with others, all around the world. He has brought me through difficult, uncertain and confusing times. Without Him, I would be nothing. He is truly my Rock and ever-present help and refuge in times of trouble.

I thank my family: Husband Paul, and daughters Myla-Danae and Malaeya for always being here for me and supporting me through the process of writing this book. I also thank my relatives and friends who have supported and encouraged me always, especially my sisters Myrna and Rhoda Louis. I love you all!

~Marlene Louis Blyden

INDEX